ABC OF PROFESSION

Visit Our Author Page
For More books like this

SCAN ME

MLOUDS
BOOKS

This Book Belongs to

A
is for
Astronaut

Explores space and conducts scientific research on space stations

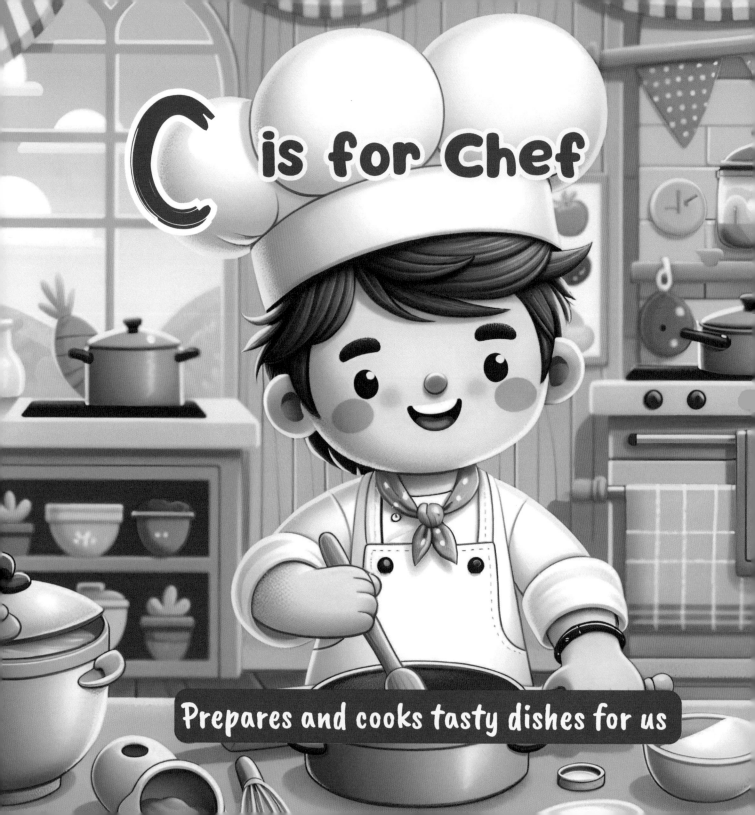

C is for Chef

Prepares and cooks tasty dishes for us

D
is for
Doctor

Provides medical care to us when we get sick

E
is for Engineer

Designs, builds, and maintains various structures and systems

F
is for
Firefighter

Extinguish fires and rescues people in emergencies

G is for Gymnast

Performs athletic activities requiring flexibility, strength, and coordination

H is for Hairstylist

Cuts and styles hair to enhance our appearance

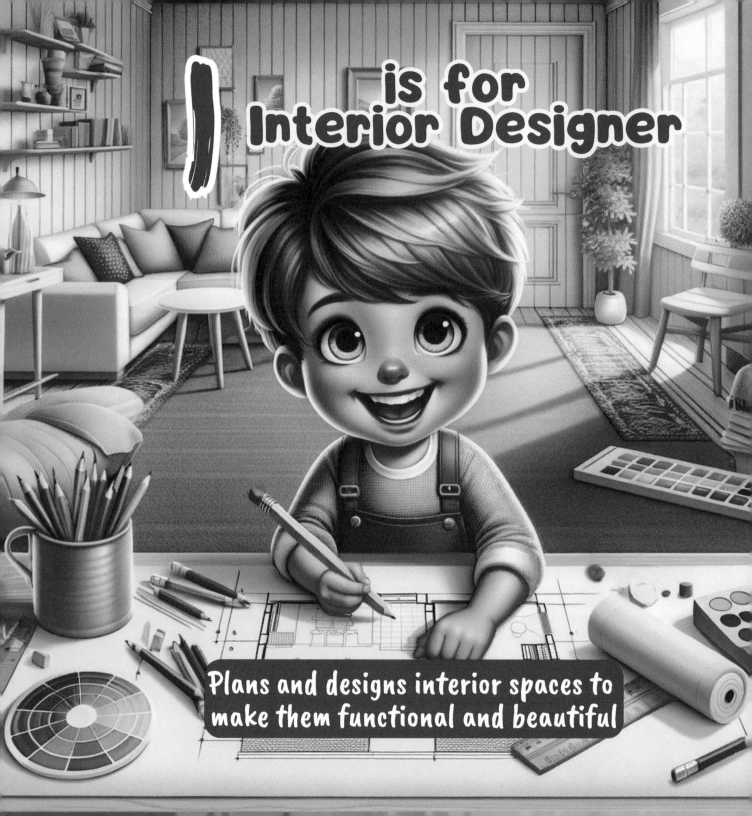

I is for Interior Designer

Plans and designs interior spaces to make them functional and beautiful

K

is for
Kindergarten
Teacher

Educates young children, fostering their development and learning

L is for Lawyer

Represents clients in legal matters and provides legal advice

M is for Musician

Sing, perform, compose, record music, and play instruments

N

is for Nurse

Provides medical care, supports patients, and assists doctors

P is for Pilot

Flies airplanes ensuring the safety of passengers

Q is for Quality Inspector

Check products and materials to ensure they meet quality standards

R
is for
Race Car
Driver

Competes in car races, aiming for speed and precision on the track

S is for Scientist

Conducts research and experiments to discover new knowledge and advance technology.

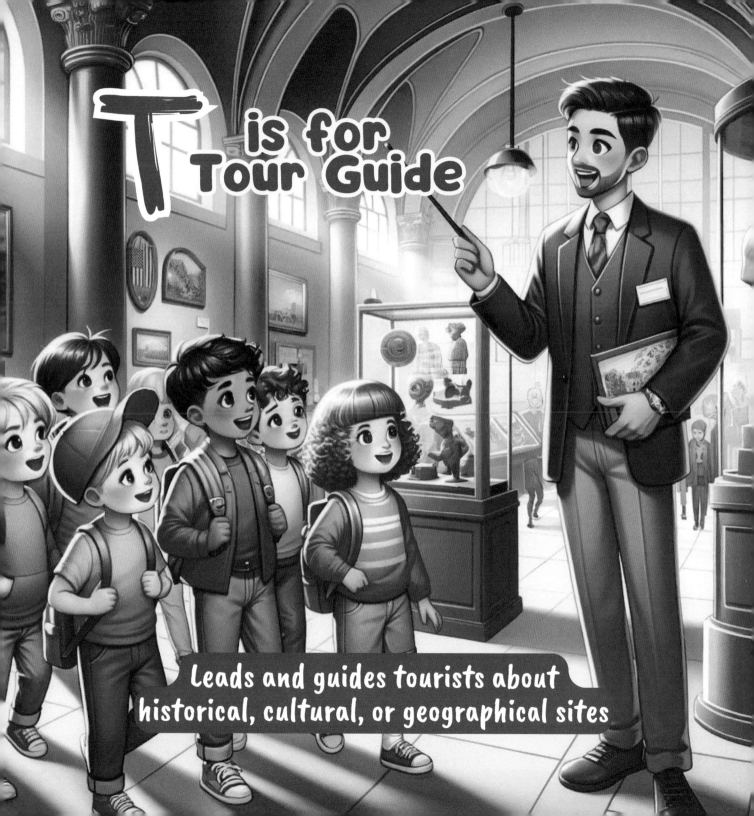

T is for Tour Guide

Leads and guides tourists about historical, cultural, or geographical sites

U is for UN Ambassador

Represents a country's interests in the United Nations, working on international relations

V
is for
Veterinarian

Provides medical care to animals when they are sick

W is for **Wildlife Photographer**

Captures images of animals and natural environment

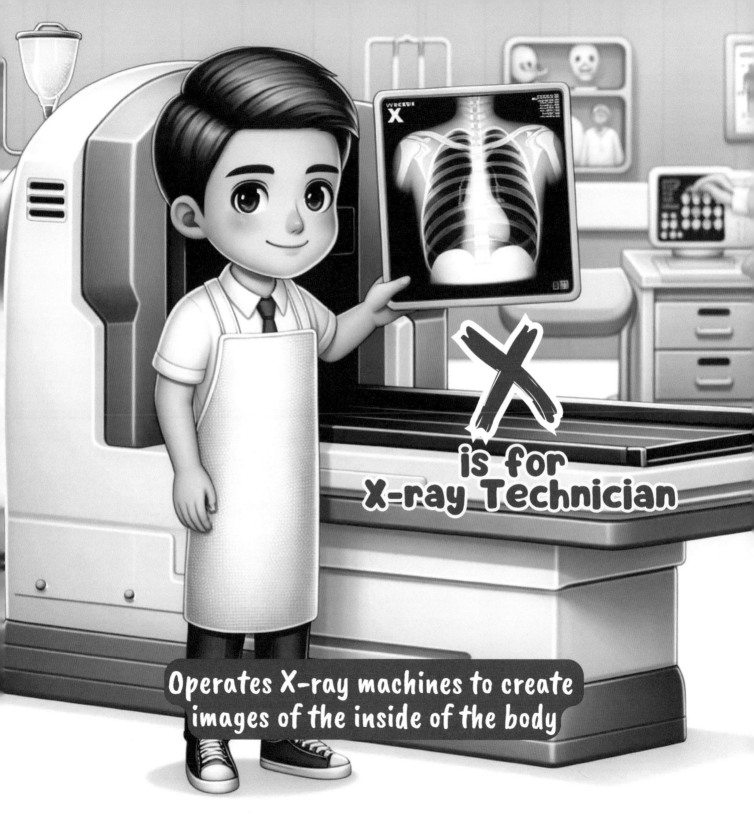

X is for X-ray Technician

Operates X-ray machines to create images of the inside of the body

Y is for Yoga Instructor

Teaches yoga, guiding students through exercises for health and relaxation

Z

is for Zoologist

Studies animals and their behavior, often in their natural habitats.

What's your Dream Job & Why?

CERTIFICATE

OF APPRECIATION

This certificate is Proudly Presented to:

_____

For Learning A to Z of Professions

_____

PARENT

Printed in Great Britain
by Amazon